RAINDROP FALLING

RAINDROP FALLING

A Westerner's journey into the center of the self

T.A. MANN

Cover Photo by Phelan Sykes
Poem by Atul Ranchod
Poem by Carla Cahill

T.A. Mann

Contents

Permission — vii
A Privilege — ix
Dedication — xi

1. KNOW THYSELF SOCRATES — 1
2. THE PARADOX BETWEEN BELIEVING AND KNOWING — 11
3. THE BEGINNING — 15
4. WHY THE HEART OF A CHILD? — 19
5. A MOST REWARDING TRANSFORMATION — 29
6. EVERYONE WANTS TO GO TO HEAVEN… BUT NO ONE WANTS TO DIE — 39
7. A SIGNIFICANT TURNING POINT — 43
8. I FOUND ANSWERS — 49
9. HOW DOES ONE GO WITHIN and WHY? — 59

10	A GREAT GIFT IS HIDDEN IN PLAIN SIGHT	77
11	LAST CHAPTER	85

My Whisper   87
About The Author   89

Permission

If this book appears to
Be alone, or loose.
This book is now yours.

A Privilege

RAINDROP FALLING

A Westerner's journey into the center of the self

It has been a privilege to live. The miracle of self-awareness is precisely that. My recognition of life enveloping my every step is truly a marvel. Time, that elusive but unyielding heartbeat of existence, is an ingredient of Life worthy of gratitude. My time here is short, and the time for me to go is growing shorter by the hour. While I am mindful and aware, I choose to devote the time I have remaining wisely. I aim to be the first patriot of the heart.

To attain Peace requires everything you have. It is not a straightforward path to follow and the road to peace is uncrowded. Very few in history have chosen to walk this direction. It requires more strength, more courage, more determination, and more clarity than preparing for war. You will never get a medal, no one will ever know your name, there will be no statues in your honor and only you will know what you have accomplished. Only you and your creator will know what you have accomplished.

Raindrop Falling is my personal journey of discovering

sanctuary within. Let me begin by saying that we hide from a great resource that has been calling our name since childhood. Although the calling of the heart is transmitted only through 'feeling' and not words. This book describes my passage to rediscover the core of the self. If you have ever felt there was more to life, I recommend turning within.

T.A. Mann

Dedication

Blessed be
For the blessing came.
It manifested and blessing
Was relentlessly reminded.
Today as anew as when
The lord of light invited you
Into his blessed realm,
With blessings without end!
The Poet Atul

Copyright © 2020 by T.A. Mann
ISBN 978-1-7344457-1-8

All rights reserved. No part of this book may be reproduced in any manner whatsoever without written permission except in the case of brief quotations embodied in critical articles and reviews.

First Printing, JUNE 2020

I

KNOW THYSELF
SOCRATES

This life is a reward. To discover the truth to this statement requires clarity, which can only be found by making an effort. This small book documents my journey to see the core of myself. It might sound weird to some but it shouldn't. Our human life is a doorway, a threshold, and I assure you it is not a metaphor. You might ask yourself why Life in the first place? To give you the option, the option to turn within and embrace Life itself.

What you are about to be introduced here might not be of any interest to you. Then again, it might resemble a feeling you have harbored but never had the words to express. The following pages describe my journey to discover an inner world waiting for me. This book introduces the claim that we hide a great gift in plain sight. This powerful resource lies just below the surface, and although this miracle is directly under one's nose, we don't perceive it. The inherent value of this resource and what it can do for us is unmeasurable.

At birth, Life included the ingredients for fulfillment tucked conveniently within each of us so we could carry our treasure with us wherever we went. But over time and the march into adulthood, we lost or traded these treasures of joy with poor substitutes that require more and more of our attention to maintain. Resulting in our inability to stop the train of thoughts in our head. To recover your treasure requires your willingness to travel inward. Inward to the center of the self. This is where the gift lives.

My name is T.A. Mann, this is my story, my discovery. This is my shout to all those that will find riches in my encouragement. I was born and raised here in America and taught our culture's rules to abide by if I wished to attain happiness. Although I was successful in attaining many accomplishments, the rewarding experience was hollow and vacant. This troubled me greatly. And so I began to reevaluate my beliefs and found that I was missing a significant ingredient in my life. This thirst to know something grew within me until I questioned most everything, hoping to find an unknown answer.

Looking back at this time of my life, I would say by just leaning in the direction to know an unknown was helpful in my discovery. This quest went against the grain of my family, friends, teachers, church, and my town. I wanted to go on pleasing everyone, but I could no longer endure the charade I had been living. When in fact, my life needed something incredible, and I honestly didn't have a clue where to find it?

This dilemma grew within me until what little happiness I had finally vacated. For eight months, I did not smile. I would wear a fake smile as a mask just so others wouldn't see the person I had become. I was healthy and ambitious and yet hollow on the inside. No matter how hard I would try, the resulting outcome was always dry and desperate. Why life became my silent mantra. The expectations for me were to complete my education, get married, have children, work until I retire, and then graciously die. Surely, there must be more to life?

Then one fortuitous day. I received a phone call from a surfing buddy I had not seen in over a year. He had something extraordinary to share with me from his travels. This encounter led to another group meeting where for the first time I listened to a melody of expressions that ignited my flame to know more. It was at this event where I heard several speakers my age sharing their personal experiences about the world within. As if there was an actual realm deep within us all. A kingdom of the heart (so to speak), where one could discover for themselves. And they expected you to discover it for yourself and not believe it.

Something deep within me resonated. It was here, while seated on the floor I became aware that I was smiling. I raised my fingers slowly to my mouth to confirm that yes; it was a smile, and it wasn't fake. Something about what I was listening to had touched me deeply. A feeling from within me was struggling to communicate great importance. Perhaps to you, a silly facial expression such as a smile to be nothing. But for me, it meant everything. This is where my pilgrimage to discover the center of myself began. I can only imagine where I would be today if I missed this seemingly uneventful moment in time.

It was at this event where I heard the following story told

by a young woman named Lynn. I never heard it repeated and have never forgotten how it affected me. Maybe it was the depth of her delivery or the unfamiliar setting but for whatever the magic was, it awakened my heart. I had waited a very long time to hear a string of words that spoke directly to me.

THE PARABLE OF AMNESIA MAN

There once was a man, for reasons unknown upon entering his sedan in haste, he bumped his head on the door's opening and collapsed into the driver's seat unconscious. When he awoke from his brief spell, something disturbing had occurred; he didn't know who he was.

In his panic, his eyes roamed the cab's interior and then rested on the center of the steering wheel. With a sigh of relief in recapturing his self-awareness, he exclaimed: "Aha! I am a Rolls-Royce!" With his misguided memory, he continued to verbally reiterate his returning awareness. "A Rolls-Royce; I am fast and smooth. I have handcrafted upholstery using Corinthian leather with burl wood details. My sweeping lines enhance my charisma. I am an automobile that is always dynamic, even when perfectly still."

After adjusting himself in the driver's seat, he started the engine, while feeling proud of how he handled his brief self-crisis. With a cocky swag of accomplishment, he put the automobile into gear and turned onto the highway.

While driving down the road, he felt the first pangs of hunger rising. He pulled off the highway and into a service station where an attendant approached. "What shall it be Sir?" said the attendant. "Filler-up!" said Amnesia Man with

Rolls-Royce hubris. The attendant performed his duties and Amnesia Man was quickly on his way. As Amnesia Man rubbed his stomach with pleasure he announced, "Ah... I'm stuffed!"

After driving for only a few miles his misguided satisfaction turned to doubt as once again while talking to himself he said. "You know, I am still hungry, actually I'm starving!" With this, he felt motivated once again to seek another service station. It wasn't long before he pulled into a bright yellow location where a cheerful fellow was waiting to serve him. "Listen, my good man. I'm starving. Fill me up!" demanded Amnesia Man using his thumb gesturing towards the back of the car. "Excuse me, Sir," said the astonished attendant with a perplexed look on his face. "I can fill up the car, but I can't fill you up."

Wow, this comment confused Amnesia Man something fierce. But because of his developed pride and ego, rather than asking the attendant to clarify his comment, Amnesia Man did the opposite and thanked him. With a fake smile and a wave of his hand, he was off again down the desert highway.

He was now driving faster as his hunger pangs were growing exponentially. The first signs of stress began as beads of sweat forming on his brow. In this bombardment of emotions, he was still trying to understand the last comment the attendant had said: "I can fill up your car but I can't fill you up." That just made no sense at all, because he was the car. Wasn't that obvious?

With the slow creep of nightfall, he approached another service station. Leaning out of the window before the attendant arrived he said; "Listen, I'm starving. I need you to fill me up as fast as possible." He blurted with only a hint of humility.

The attendant stopped in his tracks and looked suspiciously at the man leaning out of his car window. The attendant reached over to the paper dispenser, pulled down one sheet of those blue industrial napkins, removed his pen from his breast pocket, and drew something. When the attendant completed his handiwork, he turned towards Amnesia Man and presented his drawing. On the blue napkin was a rough sketch of a car with the outline of a man in the window. Pointing to the sketch of the car he said; "I can fill up the car... but I can't fill YOU up!"

"Aaahh! Thank you, thank you," said Amnesia Man, again faking he understood the attendant's description. "May I have that?" Pointing to the blue paper towel. Struggling to understand the true meaning of this valuable parchment, Amnesia Man sped back onto the highway.

He was now barreling down the highway. Scared, frustrated, and starving. He was holding a precious but mysterious blue scripture not knowing its true meaning. Amnesia Man felt lost, his hunger bent him over and his fear made him tremble uncontrollably.

After several tormenting miles, he saw something way up ahead in the darkness. It began as a speck of light. As he drew closer, the light formed the last service station. Amnesia Man pulled off the highway and approached the structure with caution. He felt he would surely perish if only disappointment awaited him. The Rolls-Royce entered the filling bay.

Amnesia Man, now timid and his voice shaking from deep

hunger and fear, turned towards the approaching attendant, and with all the sincerity and humility he could muster, pleaded: "Sir, I have traveled so very far and have not found the fulfillment I so desire. I have heard inspiring words and have collected sacred scriptures but I am no closer to finding a way out of my predicament than when I began. Please, Sir, I need your help. I have nowhere else to turn."

Maybe it was the humility in the request or the final aspiration from a suffering soul. Whatever it was, the service station attendant approached the Amnesia Man. The attendant reached gently into the open car window, past Amnesia Man's face, and gripped the rear-view mirror. The attendant gave the little mirror a gentle twist and immediately Amnesia Man was staring at his own reflection. With this simple and profound gesture, came a rush of emotions as the man realized something unbelievable and yelled, "I am the driver of the car. I am NOT the car itself! I am the Driver!"

The driver turned toward the attendant who acknowledged the man's awareness with a gentle smile and a soft gesture, pointing to a nearby roadside diner, open 24 hours. With an exchange of great thanks, the driver proceeded to the diner to have a long-awaited meal.

* * *

At birth, I bumped my head on the way out (so to speak) similar to the story of the Amnesia Man. Over time, I developed the belief that my body was all that I was. If my body was beautiful, then I was a beautiful person. If I could accomplish great things, then I must be great. But if I failed, or defeated, rejected by my peers, mocked, humiliated, victimized and abandoned — then clearly, I reflected my lot in life.

This is not true at all! There is no difference between success and failure, absolutely. The car is only the car, but it isn't you. I had traveled to every available service station (a metaphor for every person, place, or pursuit) and tried desperately to be fulfilled. I gleamed momentary whiffs of fulfillment but no amount of wealth, power, war, sex, drugs, beauty, accomplishment, and (your pursuit here) would ever be enough to fill the hole inside. The driver will eventually starve to death. Culminating in self-inflicting destruction and usually going so far as contemplating suicide.

My discovery is that our true identity is something deep within us. Our body has needs, and our true-self has needs similar to the hunger felt by the driver in the story. Knowing the driver of my car brought me a completion beyond description.

Everything we have ever needed to obtain fulfillment has always been inside of us since birth and constantly upgraded with every breath. Our life holds within it, the abundance of Life's ever-increasing resource for joy. If only we can distinguish between the driver of the car and the car itself. With this self-awareness, you will treat both with reverence and sanctity.

This sacred place within us is ours and no one else's until our last breath. This book documents my journey on the way to this discovery. This Life is a gift, or better yet a reward. Knowing the bridge to this awareness will bring you a feeling of great peace. It has for me.

The ability to go within astounds those who discover it for

themselves. Something so valuable becomes priceless to those that dare to embrace the pure nature of one's life. For me, to explore and recover my essence requires the courage of an explorer, along with the immeasurable spirit of a child.

You have the tools. We all have the tools but over time have misplaced them or discarded them. Your most prized human sense of all is your feelings, and yet we don't even recognize it as one. It is not uncommon to use this term when describing a painful event by saying, "You've hurt my feelings." This instrument of profound importance is your beacon when traveling within. Feelings are not emotions; Please don't confuse them.

Understanding the value of using one's feelings more than your thoughts is uncommon. We do the opposite. Our culture almost demands that one 'think it through' before we enact any action. We also relegate our decisions by following influencers to steer our perception rather than a self-discovery to know firsthand. We would benefit immensely to become reacquainted with our inner self. Our internal feelings are more powerful than you think. We regret it when we didn't listen to our gut after something disastrous happens. We felt the deal was too good to be true, or the person was untrustworthy but we talked ourselves into our mess by using our head and emotions. So I ask you if you intend to continue reading my story to use your feelings to guide your way.

2

THE PARADOX BETWEEN BELIEVING AND KNOWING

Imagine if you will (for a moment, humor me) that you have taken your spouse out for a fine dining experience. With your reservations securely in hand, you arrive at your desired restaurant and are escorted to your reserved table. The table setting itself is something to behold. Elegantly appointed with fine crystal, fine china, and real silverware. The centerpiece is a beautifully handcrafted, blown glass vase with a wonderfully designed flower arraignment highlighted with lit candles. Truly an experience dripping with anticipation.

Your waiter greets you with grace and elegance and describes the evening's meal especially prepared by the chef for tonight's occasion while two other waiters spread your napkins over your laps and pour water into your awaiting water glasses.

"Welcome to Chez Pierre's, I hope you will allow me to describe tonight's experience? We begin tonight's meal with something prepared to awaken your pallet made from the heart of a rare Arizona cactus drizzled with a subtle touch of jasmine puree mixed with a white wine sauce and topped with pleasure petals flown in from the Amazon delta. I will accompany each course with a wine pairing selected by our sommelier especially for you." He smiles after he completes his presentation and leaves.

Within moments, two supporting waiters arrive and remove your presentation plates and replace them with the small appetizer plates (obviously in preparation for the heart of cactus). You and your spouse enjoy each other's company while you patiently await the continuation of the evening's meal.

Our waiter returns and begins joyfully to describe tonight's salad that is being prepared and goes into minute detail describing the leaf and the mixture of vegetables along with the dressing the chef has created for you... Then he leaves once again.

The two supporting waiters return and remove the appetizer plates and replace them with salad plates along with the accompanying silverware. After some 15 minutes, our waiter returns and describes the soup that is being prepared for tonight's meal in exquisite detail that only heightens your hunger and anticipation.

And yet, this whole time, no bread, no wine, no heart of cactus, no salad, no soup, just one beautifully detailed description, one after another, right through the main course and into the desert description along with the selected wine pairing. You sat there for nearly two hours in each other's company, albeit missing the entire fine dining experience.

Our waiter makes one final appearance as he places the check for tonight's meal. When you confront the waiter and ask, "Where is the food?" he responds with shock, "You only need to 'Believe' that this meal exists for it to fulfill you". Would you object to this argument? Would you pay money for this? And yet, this is exactly what we do in our lives.

We allow our culture to describe the coming of great things and convince ourselves that we only need to believe for all of it to manifest. We find this pattern everywhere. From our politicians that promise wondrous new beginnings if only you would vote for them. From career guidance counselors to military recruitment officers to time-share salesmen along with reverse mortgage advisors and investment brokers. Every TV commercial subjects us to a finely crafted call to believe their story. Believe in the product, believe in this cruise, and believe the newscaster. We are surrounded by beliefs. Even in our churches and synagogues require the congregation to believe for the promise of the afterlife. If you want to change global warming, we believe our scientist will discover a solution. God forbid I will need to change my lifestyle.

We live with beliefs, hopes, and dreams, and many, many promises. We tell ourselves that yes, we can make a difference all the while praying to win the lottery so we can cover up our disappointments and accept replacement killers; Indulgence, and amorality. When does Knowing become paramount over Believing? When does it occur to you that everything someone has taught you to believe was just a belief? Spooky isn't it when you see how expansive it is in our culture?

Knowing something requires action. You need to confirm an intuition for the knowledge to be real. For example, ask yourself if there are any beers in your refrigerator right now? You need to get off the sofa, pull your face away from watching the TV, move your person into the kitchen, open the refrigerator door to acknowledge that yes, there are beers in my refrigerator. Belief just won't bring fulfillment of beer, will it? You need to make all those decisions along with those actions to emphatically know for sure that yes, there is beer in the refrigerator and even then, you still need to bend over and reach within the cool air of the open door, grab a cold beer, and lift it free by using the muscles in your body to pull the beer out. You must physically twist the cap off and raise the bottle to your lips and pour ever so slightly into your mouth to enjoy the fruits of your discovery. That is the difference between believing and knowing. One takes an exceptional amount of determination and effort to fulfill. The other is only make-believe.

Why did I write this elaborate chapter? Gaining the true knowledge of the self requires you to make more effort than you have ever made before. Similar to any endeavor, it demands everything from you at first, but over time your desire to rediscover will make your efforts natural. One cannot help themselves from indulging in clarity. Know Thyself, is not a metaphor. The Kingdom of Heaven is within, is not an analogy.

3

THE BEGINNING

Where does it begin? The awareness you have a hunger. Regardless of what you do to quell its pang, it does not go away. For me, it was a combination of personal life events coming to a tipping point. And then one night, after returning from a late-night party, while staring at my reflection in the bathroom mirror. It hit me; I feel worse than before the evening's event. I had gained no heartfelt celebration from my attendance. I would have been better off if I had stayed home and cooked beans. It was only a few weeks earlier; I had become a national award winner and yet I felt less successful than before my victory. My friends would tell me "You're the Man" and yet somehow my heart didn't agree with their admiration.

In reflection, I had accomplished what our society holds in high regard, but the resulting feeling I was expecting wasn't there. I had gained acceptable amounts of wealth, the respect of my family, the position at work, and the athletic ability to do almost anything. Yet with all my blessings, the driver of the car was starving to death. Regardless of the support from my family and friends along with the number of achievements, I still couldn't deliver a smile to my face. Have you ever felt like this?

Here I was at 2:00 am staring at my reflection in the bathroom mirror feeling less fulfilled then I tell myself. It was a great party, everyone was there and that sexy girl gave me her number. And yet as I stand here, I cannot bullshit myself. I cannot put on another fake smile. I feel internally starved with no hope on the horizon.

The odd thing is, I am doing everything according to my culture's bylaws. They taught me that if I do this and this along with that, the combination will bring me overwhelming joy. And yet, it is simply not so. It feels hollow as if I am the king with new clothes (the Aesop fable). Here I am parading around in my underwear with not a stitch of substance. I have taken my car to every gas station and have had my fill, only to feel awkwardly separated further and further from the internal gong that confirms that I have arrived.

For me, it began with the slightest recognition of an internal voice. It is a little voice, a voice deep within us. In all honesty, this beautiful voice does not speak. It cannot because its nature is to make no sounds at all. All it can do is FEEL. One reason we cannot hear it is because over time we have been conditioned to only listen to the loudest voice in the room or our head.

This wonderful voice, the one that only feels, is your truest and oldest friend. When you were young, the two of you were inseparable. You only knew what you felt and not what you thought. You were a feeling life-form full of passion for living. Every day was an 'Anything Can Happen Day'. You would never sleep in late, or felt fat, or skinny, or felt old. To you, the summer months lasted for years! The week before Christmas was the most painful week to endure because it lasted forever. And you couldn't remember yesterday if your life depended on it. You and your little voice felt your way through life.

Now we are older and we've exchanged feelings for thoughts. We refrain from remembering some thoughts because it stirs up emotions we don't want to revisit. Now we think a lot more. We think so much that we cannot stop thinking and use devices to drown out the voices in our heads. The music in the car is loud, the TV is loud, we talk loud, we laugh loud and we think and think and think. We know how to navigate the politics at work and trust very few. We don't trust our family members and for good reasons most of the time. We have a glass of wine or a puff in the evenings to wind down. We do less creative things and engage less with others just so we can veg or decompress from the day. We take pills to help us sleep because we are still uncontrollably thinking. And I am sure we have not felt that little voice since puberty.

This is where it began for me, with an internal inventory mixed with unfulfilled aspirations. I feel that all of us in our youth made an unconscious vow to achieve fulfillment. We might have different translations resulting in our ideal of that achievement. Some craved to become rich while others wanted to be tall and beautiful. I dreamt to make the Olympics, but what I was aspiring for was not the result but the feeling of the result.

It has always been the feeling of success, the feeling of accomplishment, and the feeling of love I so desperately pursued. It will consistently be an internal feeling that answers our call. A simple yet vast intensity. It sounds childlike, doesn't it? But that elusive quality is exactly what we are starving for. At least it was with me. A profound, bigger than one's self, kind of experience.

It never occurs to our logic mind that fulfillment lies within. We carry this precious alloy with us. One needs only a means of traveling within to tap the resource we were born with. If I am crippled, paralyzed, and blind, but still breathing. The means to swim in the ocean of joy is mine if I know the path within. Our life is incredibly profound.

I struggled with the difference between feeling and thinking. Quickly recognizing feelings to be a million times more valuable and necessary. Would you fight off a thief determined to steal your car? Maybe, maybe not. Would you engage fiercely if that thief was stealing fulfillment from you? Which one is worthy of your fight?

This understanding of the significance of feelings becomes a driving force. Recognize real strength from the false substitute. Over time, we have grown to accept the unreal substitutes in our lives, where we have discarded joy for authority. Where we have replaced kindness with leverage and knowing gives way to believing. The beginning is when we want to find a direction that will reward ourselves with a FEELING for every step we take.

4

WHY THE HEART OF A CHILD?

Because when we were children we explored our surroundings using our feelings. Our thinking mind didn't become dominant until around puberty or if some life-altering event has taken place. To travel within one's self requires you to adopt feelings as your compass (not emotions). And if you are like me, recovering my feeling ability is challenging. I keep relying on my logic and thinking mind to lead me. Which always ends with disastrous results.

It is this strength that children have to morph and adapt to almost any circumstance that will serve you going inward. It is a discovery that you are embarking on and the only way to find this realm is by using your feelings (I will say this boldly). As I sit here writing this paragraph, my chest is humming with a strong and relentless feeling. Yeah, you try to describe it to someone. This feeling nature that you possess is a miracle. You can use your sense of feeling in all aspects of life. Inward and outward.

Several incredible artists could imbue feeling into their art. Don't believe me? The next time you are near a real Van Gogh painting. Turn your back to the art hanging there. Have a friend guide you across the floor slowly, and using only your feelings, tell your friend when you think the painting is directly behind you. Your feelings will place you directly in front of the painting. As if two magnets were making the connection. Now, how did he do that?

The heart of a child is also amazingly brave. The challenge you are on will require bravery, a lot of it. There is nothing monstrous, but going deep will reveal elements of yourself that require an amount of fortitude to continue. The strength and durability of a child's heart become instrumental in your journey. Perhaps it is the nature of discovery, the way a child will begin their day with that awe-inspiring pursuit to discover and discover more. The child only knows what they feel, whereas an adult, only knows what they think. It is the heart of a child that will carry you further with an ever-increasing ability to absorb more.

THE STORYTELLER

Our story opens on a well-lit Kindergarten classroom in an ordinary suburban neighborhood. The class is taught by two female schoolteachers, Beverly and Caryn. Beverly, the senior, has been with the school for years while Caryn's teaching career has only begun.

Amongst the chaos of kinders in this classroom stands

Beverly who is informing the adorable monsters they have a special guest today; Saffron the Storyteller! The normal audio level of the class immediately erupts to a heightened decibel range upon hearing Saffron's name. This outpouring of excitement startles Caryn, witnessing the reaction from this simple announcement.

Beverly continues to direct the massing herd to prepare for Saffron's arrival. With her command and the wave of her hand, the children frantically rush to rearrange chairs and cushions, painting projects and artboards, all to make space for the storyteller. Caryn is standing towards the back of the room next to the small appliance counter, preparing a hot cup of Earl Grey tea as Beverly joins her. Recognizing Caryn's curiosity with this monumental announcement, she informs Caryn what she should expect.

"Saffron is a storyteller. He is fantastic! The children just love the man and always look forward to his visits. Every one of his stories is extraordinary, and he never repeats himself. I don't know how he does it. He will keep them intrigued until the bell for recess."

Beverly continues; "Caryn, I need to run to the library and keep working on the newsletter for a time... so stay with the children; introduce yourself to Saffron when he arrives; he is a nice man, you will like him. I will catch up with you when I return after recess." And with that, Beverly is out the door.

Within moments after Beverly's departure, there is a metallic tap on the classroom door. The kind of sound that resonates if one was to use the metal head of a walking cane or perhaps a solid ring. Caryn is watching someone quietly entering the room. This must be the storyteller she assumes.

With all the noise associated with the preparation, no one has noticed Saffron's entrance. Saffron appears to be patiently and calmly scanning the chaos in the room and spreads a smile on his face watching the children and their exciting activity. His gaze finally finds Caryn standing by the kitchenette and moves in her direction.

Instantly, the children realize that Saffron has arrived and charge to mob him as only kinders can. The children are swarming amid his welcoming arms. The audio level in the room has reached new heights while the children pull and tug for his attention. As he floats towards Caryn with this torrent of children, he greets her with a friendly theatrical bow. The audio level of this joyful moment requires him to yell over the roar of the children. "Hi, I'm Saffron, your storyteller!"

Saffron's youth catches Caryn by surprise. He isn't old, gray, or disheveled, but quite the opposite. He stands straight and moves with grace. He has a boyish smile that playfully warms you. "Hello Saffron, my name is Caryn! I hear you are a gifted storyteller!" As she reaches out to shake his hand. "I'm sorry but Beverly couldn't be here. She had to do some work on the school's newsletter. So, it's just me... for your story hour."

Saffron smiles and nods with understanding, but his attention is now following the children gathering themselves on the carpet eagerly waiting for the story hour to begin. Saffron motions to Caryn for her permission to begin. And without hesitation, Caryn returns her gesture of approval. Saffron turns away from Caryn and glides to the front of the room. Towering over all the shining faces, he looks down with a funny smirk. "Shall we visit someplace new today?" "YES!"

Scream the children, followed by a cacophony of laughter from this fluid pool of children.

Caryn reaches for her cup of tea and leans against the counter in anticipation of the story to begin. Saffron moves over a small children's wooden stool in front and lowers himself down onto this little perch. His knees almost reach the height of his chin. As soon as he leans in towards the children... all the noise in the room goes dead silent. This abrupt reaction from the children startles Caryn. She has never seen this expression coming from children in her life. This man surely must be the Pied Piper himself. The only sound noticeable in the room is the gentle clinking sound coming from Caryn's teacup while she stirs with a metal spoon.

Saffron closes his eyes in a motionless state of being as if he is preparing the perfect adventure for the day. The children are about to pop with their anticipation. It appears as if this union between the children and Saffron is causing the room to grow even quieter. The silence is so heavy, Caryn feels she can hear music.

After a sustained period, Saffron begins his story with a whisper of a voice, requiring one to strain a little to hear his opening lines. An overwhelming hypnotic vacuum appears to be building and, if possible, slowing time itself.

Caryn slowly raises her cup of Earl Grey preparing to take her first sip when suddenly something makes her stop in midair. She is experiencing something she wouldn't know how to explain. It requires all of her composure not to scream or drop her teacup. She is staring in disbelief as the schoolroom wall immediately behind Saffron is escaping brick-by-brick, each one is being pulled into a black hole. In two blinks of an eye, the wall, the ceiling, and the floor have all given way to a vast desert-scape with camels, horses, dunes, and a magnificent desert oasis way off in the distance. She instantly feels the waft of the hot desert air caressing her face, which causes her to blink in disbelief. Only to be seduced with the fragrance of her surroundings as she inhales without an end. What just happened? Where in the world am I? What is this enchanted place?

Her gaze is still on Saffron as he stands up and takes a pose. In another timeless moment, Caryn is watching Saffron physically transform himself into a dark-skinned desert sheik. He now has a magnificent black beard and wears a beautiful blue silk turban with matching flowing robes, along with a bejeweled-encrusted sword that he wears in his gold-embroidered waistband.

Suddenly in a burst of awareness, she remembers the children and desperately tries to locate them in this foreign land. To her surprise, this magic doesn't scare them at all. Rather, they appear to embrace this realm with ease or were already expecting this transformation to occur. They, too, are wearing clothing of different characteristics to play their part within Saffron's story-world. One young girl, Jennifer, has comfortably settled into what appears to be a desert hunter wearing a beautiful flowing gown with a magnificent hunting falcon on her leather-gauntlet wrist. Jennifer is admiring her beautiful raptor on her arm and sees Caryn staring at her. Jennifer gestures with a smile as she proudly displays her falcon.

Several other children in costume are resting peacefully on an arrangement of stacked silk pillows on a beautiful Persian rug spread out over the sand and listening intently to Saffron's voice in this enchanted place.

Saffron is spinning a magical tale that goes straight to Caryn's heart with such deliberate intent. She cannot resist the overtures of this adventure, her inhibitions freely give way to this ethereal realm. She feels her feet sink into the sand as she watches herself transforming into character. Every intoxicating breath from this blessed sanctuary feels so right.

The storyteller weaves a narrative about the love between a prince and his beloved. How a jealous and greedy king jeopardizes that love, and what they must do to find courage and bravery. The children scream and shriek at every turn in Saffron's fable. The story continuously evolves and so does the surroundings. Time and space appear to be mere settings transforming and morphing at will. The harmony of Saffron's magical voice is weaving every passage of the story into the texture of this enchanted land. And just when Caryn is about to lose herself completely... swoosh! It all returns to normal.

The story's epic conclusion hurtles Caryn back into reality, back into the classroom to the eruption of applause and cheering from the adoring children. Most of the children are screaming; "This was the best story ever!" Caryn is struggling between two worlds. What happened to my beautiful clothes and all of my gold jewelry I was wearing? Where is my horse I was riding? Wasn't it dark just moments ago? We were outside under that sensual canopy of stars. What happened to those incredible musicians that were playing...? Was this all a dream?

The school bell rings announcing the time for recess. As Saffron stands up, the children swarm under him to usher him out into the playground as an honored guest. Caryn is dumbstruck. She is still holding her cup of Earl Grey in the same location where it all began; she doesn't know what to say. Caryn's attention is quickly diverted to the fragrance leftover in her hair. She quickly pulls her hair over her nose and inhales, only to catch the last fleeting breath of perfume to confirm, it wasn't a dream... it was real.

As Saffron drifts past Caryn, he recognizes the condition she has found herself in. He appears to be happily surprised and cheers, "Why Caryn, you still have a heart of a child, magical, isn't it?" As he floats with the bubbling current of children out into the playground. He looks back towards Caryn and giggles with a child-like smile.

* * *

Why is it the older we become we still feel youthful? Although we are aware of our aging, we still embrace youthful challenges. Dirt bike riding, pier jumping, rock climbing, big wave surfing, skydiving, and many physical challenges we did in our youth are now viewed as dangerous risks even though we would love to do them one more time. My grandmother on her death bed told me she still feels as if she is in her 20's. Yet she knows by looking at her body she is an old lady. I never forgot that exchange. For me, the driver is ageless, while the car ages and decays. Knowing the driver keeps us feeling young and full.

As adults, we rarely use the word joy in our vocabulary. Children exude joy almost daily. Joy is a fleeting experience, a rapture of the heart, a beautiful word that describes a true feeling. Experiencing joy will stop time in its tracks. Joy makes you feel intoxicated. The influence of joy will inspire you to dance or sing out loud! Joy is nothing short of a true miracle. Joy is a brief encounter with the divine. One cannot experience joy without feeling humble. It is as rare and varied as snowflakes. One cannot trap, bottle, or imprison joy; nor can one duplicate it regardless of how hard one tries. Joy is the essence of true freedom. Joy has no age and no age discrimination. When exposed to it, joy will reduce you to a child with open arms. Joy has no form, no restrictions, and no rules. Joy is elusive and yet still omnipresent. There is no limit to how much joy one can both receive and contain. Every person is a perfect vessel to experience joy. Joy is never jealous or judgmental, regardless of whether you are a sinner or a saint. If you reduce yourself to a humble servant, joy will be your constant companion.

All of us were born with the heart of a child. We still have it; we just can't readily recall this early perception. Children, regardless of their nationality or family's religion, all want to feel valuable, capable, and loved. These three ingredients are still inherent within us. We inspire to contribute valuably to our surroundings. We desire to be capable enough to use our skills and gifts. And we dearly long to feel loved, a real love that isn't dependent on our performance or public statue. Children also have a remarkable acceptance to change. Likely stemming from their natural ability to live in the now. When they encounter something new, they use their feelings as receptors and usually without fear will voice their observation publically. "Uncle Charlie smells."

You will need the strength of a child to endure the relentless force that keeps us away from simplicity. I don't know any other way to describe it. Pure and perfect is very, very difficult. Yet, so wonderful to experience.

5

A MOST REWARDING TRANSFORMATION

THE CRAFTSMAN

AUDIO: AUSTRALIAN ACCENT FOR BOTH INDIVIDUALS

ORIGINAL STORY BY T.A. MANN DESIGNED AS AN ANIMATED SHORT SERIES.

JULY 11, 2004

Opening close-up shot: Bicycle wheel and barefoot of young boy peddling with motivation.

The camera cuts to close up of front-wheel turning this way and that navigating through small-town circa the early 1950s. Entering a local lumberyard and navigating through the stacks of lumber and local carpenters picking up their morning lumber.

The boy weaves in and out of lumber trucks and men stacking lumber. We see the boy coming to a stop while straddling his bike asking one of the lumber workers something.

The man leans over to hear attentively and then rises up and points off into the distance while nodding his head, reassuring the boy that who he is seeking is indeed present and located "over there".

Pointing to the far corner of the lumberyard where the Mill is located and where our story begins.

Voice over: As I approached him he was busy assembling and preparing wood for what looked like a door or table.

"Hello, Sir" I cautiously greeted him.

He turned his head without removing his hands from his work and with a quick nod of his head and a smile of kindness that I had grown to admire, he acknowledged me "My young apprentice."

He never called me that before and it made me feel welcomed. As I slid myself up onto a vacant work table I asked; "I've been thinking of what you said and I've come to ask you some more questions, if that is okay with you?"

He never stopped working on what was in front of him and quickly and gently responded "Where does your question come from?" in a rhetorical delivery.

That question stopped my momentum and in that pregnant pause, I replied "From within me" hoping it was the answer he was leading to. "And how will you know if your question has been answered?" he said with a glance.

This was similar to how all our meetings began; I would

start, he would set the sincerity, if I acknowledged the sincerity he would tell me things that would make my ears tingle as if I had waited my whole life to hear such words. Although I knew he spoke English, I had never heard anyone string such words together that made time standstill.

"I would be able to feel it" I replied. He grinned as if I had recognized the appropriate word Feel. "You would feel it within you" he completed my answer as I nodded with agreement. "If all answers lie within you, then you can answer your questions... Rely on your feelings to guide you."

You have to remember he never stopped working on what he was doing, always moving at the same deliberate pace and yet totally engaged with me. Sometimes he would look into my eyes but mostly he would just keep his rhythm without any disturbance or imbalance. The craftsman continued;

"Is wealth an amount of money or a feeling?"

"Is security a bodyguard or a feeling?"

"Is relaxation a vacation or a feeling?"

"Can you hold achievement in your hands, or put courage away in a safe? These are all words that we use to substitute for the actual feeling... and without the feeling, no number of accomplishments or acquired gold will fill the hole within us left by the space reserved only for feeling."

"What about the words; success, accomplishment, gratitude, perseverance, achievement, or even the word fulfillment, these words also describe feelings don't they?" With this, I nodded yes.

"Where is the location of our feelings?" "Are they owned and distributed by others?" "Or do they reside within us... perhaps in a location that at first seems distant and unattainable but with reassurance and perseverance the location becomes familiar and precious?"

"When you pursue where the heart is you will enter the source of all feelings!" he said with a glint of all-knowing and a sideways smile. "For if all answers lie within you, then you contain all the answers to your questions". "You just need to reach deeper to find the answers".

He had been sanding an assembly of fine wood that was laid out on his workbench in an orderly fashion. He put down his tools and said;

"When you are hungry what do you seek?"

"Food," I said.

"When you are cold what do you pursue?"

"A coat or a jumper" I replied.

"...And when you are thirsty?"

"A drink of water!" I replied confidently.

"Similarly, if you have a longing to feel fulfillment it will only be attained by those who pursue fulfillment...

It is no different than the banker who pursues wealth.

The celebrity who pursues fame.

The athlete who pursues excellence."

"Life gives us what we pursue but not all pursuits will bring us fulfillment.

"If you pursue joy with feeling, then you will search for the source of joy. And keep searching until your heart tells you that you have successfully acquired what you were searching for..." (the boy finishes the sentence) "If all answers lie within us than the direction to acquire the source of feelings is also within us".

The craftsman warmly smiles and lets out an easy chuckle

at the boy's enlightenment and says "Why yes it is." The Craftsman turns, reaches for a sanding block and gestures for the boy to come closer to help him with his work. The boy breaks into a smile of his own and leaps off the bench eager to help.

The End.

*writer's note: this is designed to be a serial episode where every time the two are together, kindness and wisdom unfolds.

* * *

I have witnessed that Life has a way of communicating with us. Not in words, so much, but with visible allegories. Consider the transformation of the butterfly. I look at this little pilgrim as an analogy for my personal growth and discovery. I have always felt that this little worm has no idea what the future lies ahead. An irresistible natural drive is compelling him or her forward to an unknown future. Our pilgrim will seek a suitable branch and begin spinning its cocoon. After some time in incubation, our worm is transformed into a butterfly with abilities and perceptions that far exceed its previous incarnation. The butterfly's new perception of life has evolved considerably.

Similarly, this little worm reflects me rediscovering my true self. I now have a perspective of life that I never had before. Without the cocoon, no transformation can occur. To see something hidden in plain sight is an epiphany that is so profound and yet so, so simple.

When I first started down this internal path of discovery, I was expecting something similar to an LSD experience.

Do you remember what happened to Dave in 2001 A Space Odyssey when he entered the monolith? That was my concept. Here I am, all buckled up and bracing for my transformation to occur. "Come-on butterfly, I'm ready!" I was looking for a sign of affirmation based on my developed imagination, coupled with every film on the subject, every spiritual book I ever read, and all the inspiring poets that moved me. I anticipated an experience based in a world of make-belief. What a fantasy.

I was unaware of the subtle transformation that was occurring. My daily practice to go within was uneventful (so I thought). I would sit and mostly think through my session and when I got up, I felt a little let-down that nothing incredible had erupted. No trumpets, no 10,000 suns, no past-life revelation, no mystic door opening with some glowing saint welcoming me. Even though my morning routine continued for days, I didn't see any results.

Until one day, when I went for a walk on the beach. Wow, what a BEAUTIFUL DAY!!! Thinking to myself what a spectacular afternoon this was when I passed another beachgoer walking in the opposite direction. A young woman enveloped in anguish. She was not having the same remarkable day that I was having, and then it hit me. Is it an exquisite day? Or am I feeling exquisite within me? I stopped and noticed something peculiar. I wasn't thinking. There was no chatter inside my head. What a rush! I felt like a little kid. I could feel everything around me. The water caressing my feet. The smell of the salty air. I began to have an overwhelming emotion of gratitude. Wow, what an elegant experience I was having. I had my first experience where a quiet mind allows a human to experience life unfolding. I told myself to curtail my LSD concepts and attempt to walk with my hands open so to speak. I came to understand that what I am looking for will appear new and unlimited. The memory of that afternoon is still a treasure for me. Similar to having a smile on one's face. The awareness to appreciate a moment can be a momentous occasion.

It is odd how we identify our existence. We pigeonhole ourselves by our education, profession, and monetary worth. We use the dollar amount we annually receive along with the company of friends we keep or associate with as value monikers. We parade ourselves in public similar to the King's new clothes story but with different attributes. Our jewelry choices, the cars we drive, the property we own, the clubs we are members to, the college we graduated from, the quality of our shoes and handbags, the beauty or hotness of our significant other, and yet we stand naked and afraid. These attributes are great examples of the car but not of the driver.

We struggle with rewarding ourselves with love, unconditional love. Meaning, no performance or service or action required to be drunk with love. The turning point in one's life is when you value inner love over the external substitute. The day you value yourself by the amount of unconditional passion flowing through you will be a great day. At that moment, you can freely make the statement: "I am not the car, I am the driver of the car!"

The creator did the most wonderful thing. This magnificent architect put everything that a human would require within all of us. We contain the wisdom, the wonder, and the overabundant source of love. We contain passion, bravery, and the desire to aspire. Everything that would make this life historically magnificent is within us all. And when you make this discovery on your own, believing not required, your life takes on new meaning.

How do you show your gratitude for something as great as this? By indulging in it! You show your appreciation through your expression of gratitude. No exchange of money expected. No building of temples involved or taking long pilgrimages. No need to perform rituals and austerities. One needs only to appreciate every single moment. Like a child, laughter and joy become the best language of gratefulness. There is no better way to illustrate your gratitude.

I HAD A DREAM LAST NIGHT WE WERE THE BREATH

As if by some miraculous design it was all, one Breath. And we were part and partial to that one. We were the Breath in a multitude of unique and perfectly shaped forms and very aware that we were not separate beings at all. We were all standing in grand appreciation gazing out through our forms at one another when we felt with a mixture of curiosity and discovery to search for other forms of the Breath.

It was the birds that caught our attention when high above they appeared to be experiencing the same global awakening as they flew in joyous patterns no longer separated by family flocks. Collectively their songs were a symphony to experience.

Next, it was our domestic pets that drifted towards us wearing an amazed look of joy. It was the snap of a branch, the rustle of something large approaching, and with some trepidation at first but quickly replaced with childlike anticipation the animals of the forest came out of their secluded hiding with the acknowledgment they too were also having the same self-awareness as we.

We were all the Breath in all our amazing forms and completely assuredly aware that we were not different or alone. Bears, wolves, foxes, raccoons, beavers, gophers, snakes, turtles. We were no longer hiding from one another or endangering each other either. We were in Breath.

The little field mouse with his big ears was embracing the snake and both of them were looking at each other as if reuniting with an old lost friend they hadn't seen in a very long time, and they smiled. They were the Breath. Everyone was standing motionless looking for more displays of the Breath when out crawled the bugs, lizards, snails, spiders, and those little itty-bitty ants. All around us flew moths of every shape and size along with butterflies, dragonflies, lightning bugs, and anything and everything that moved at night. Everyone was experiencing complete adulation.

At that moment a passage of wind made its presence felt with the joyous rustle touching every flower, leaf, and blade of grass causing the branches of the trees to add to the serenade when we realized it wasn't the wind; it was the Breath, and it had always been here with us. The movement along the ground causing particles to jump into the air, little dust devils danced that became a ballet of the heart. The feeling as it caressed our hair and moved gently across our face, how it ruffled our clothing, fluffed the fur on our coats, and played on our wings expressing love with such magnificence it curled our comprehension.

All of us and I mean all of us exactly at the same time wanted to express our recognition and appreciation for this experience and so in unison, we took a much appreciated slow deep breath causing our eyes to close, feeling the boundless love it was carrying, accepted that love and released it. As if by the simple gesture of accepting and recognizing the breath we were acknowledging the magnificence on having the awareness we are the Breath. Life is good.

6

EVERYONE WANTS TO GO TO HEAVEN... BUT NO ONE WANTS TO DIE

Why do you think that is? Not animals, not fish or birds or bugs, or even slimy things. No living creature large or small, young or old wants to die. Why should we object to death so violently if we BELIEVE that all living creatures have a destiny after death? Where does the 'will' to live come from? Is it possible some instinct rooted deep within all of us is screaming for recognition? Screaming for us to perceive something hidden in plain sight? Possibly begging for us to experience the magnificence within us all? Perhaps to witness and take part in something incredible?

We are living a symbiotic relationship with Life. We never consider that Life to be conscious and aware of us do we? We rarely try to communicate with Life. Without this being, we die, plain and simple. With this being, we become something remarkable. Although sadly, we approach life as if it were disposable. A fuel to use and discard. Something to step over and ignore. We chew up resources as if they were ours to devour. We hunt animals, fish, and fowl for sport and monetary gain. We pollute, condemn, and otherwise destroy. Why do we do this? What is so destructive within us that compels us to act accordingly? Why do we ignore Life?

We move through life. Life surrounds us. Life is within us. We breathe life constantly and yet are unaware of Life as a living and conscious entity. Life is within everything, regardless of whether it is mammal, rock, chemical, plant, fish, bug, or vapor. Our very being is a borrowed vessel for Life to live through us. Life was here before we arrived and will be here long after we leave and that goes for the whole human race and everything in between. The sticky point here is the awareness between ourselves and our benefactor. As soon as we acknowledge Life as a real entity, we see it everywhere and in everything. We also marvel at the display of Life as it appears to express with unlimited creativity such marvels as sunsets, breaking waves, desert flowers, moving clouds, a campfire, rain, rainbows, snowflakes, dappled shade, and on and on. Life takes on a larger significance when it no longer becomes disposable.

The most precious gift ever created, the source of all art, music, and poetry, the conqueror of all your fears, the source of love, the resource for courage, bravery and fortitude, the library of great wisdom, the most loving individual, and the rarest of beings - is YOU. You are that one precious being that only comes once in CREATION. See for yourself who you truly are. Value your existence with gratitude. Don't believe this statement; see it personally first hand. You must see it first-hand.

All your appreciation, all your gratitude, all your passion comes from within you. The source of all feeling, the origin of love, the source of joy, the source of strength, and hope is within you. It is You, the real you, not the automobile you on the outside but it is the one that people feel and the one they will miss when you have left this vehicle. You owe it to yourself to see who you truly are face to face. You have always dreamt that there was something more, and that dream becomes a reality when you are in the company with the Self.

Your path is one of a kind, the only one in history from the time immemorial. This is your path, your discovery, your Self. This is the direction to meet and embrace the driver of the car; YOU. Are there obstacles? Oh, boy! Are there ever? But when the fragrance of the Self fills your nostrils, you will want to run! You will not allow any obstacle in your way from being a hindrance.

WINDOWSILL BY THE SHORE

Setting: A young woman sitting quietly on the windowsill of an open window looking out over dunes with the shoreline beyond. She appears to be absorbing the stillness with the ocean breeze caressing her. The camera tracks over her shoulder from behind (she is facing outward) and moves around to her profile as she sits on the open window frame. As the glow of the afternoon sun reflects on her radiant face, she begins to speak.

"I wanted to see God, face-to-face. I wanted to be in His presence and to feel His majesty. Some describe Him as omnipotent, omniscient, and omnipresent. He is everywhere and in everything and nothing exists without Him I am told. To ask for help, I went to see the village Magi, and he said to call Him by his true name; Life. And when I did, I saw Life everywhere. I saw Life in everything, and I became fully aware when I breathed Life in."

She completes this last line slowly inhaling a breath, milking the experience for all its worth. She turns ever so slightly towards the camera and says; "Behold, Life!" And leaves us with a gentle all-knowing smile.

7

A SIGNIFICANT TURNING POINT

An ancient scripture describes the human condition as two birds separated on a branch. The bird that is facing outwards does not have the awareness to turn around. The other bird (the genuine love) is just out of reach behind the other but unable to get the attention of the bird upfront. The bird facing outwards is constantly calling for its genuine love (which is the one directly behind it) but sadly, only substitutions parade before it. This genuine love only has eyes for you and begs that one day you will turn around to see it. This genuine love can only radiate a feeling towards you. It cannot speak or call or do anything other than FEEL in your direction. For that is its nature.

This scripture describes that it is with a profound grace that gives this desperate beckoning bird the awareness and the strength to turn around and see the lover it has always searched for. The path of fulfillment and discovery begins here. Do you want to experience a joy you can never properly describe? Start here by embracing the love within. Because when embracing the heart, you see this world differently. Life as you thought you knew; is nothing compared to the Life conscious of you.

We do not teach this idea of an inner self and how to attain such clarity in school. Your family never shared this valuable information. It is something you will feel privately and feel you must. To make a decisive change, you need to announce to yourself that you have no choice but to find the path of fulfillment. This path is for you alone and will be the path that no one else will ever see. There will be no genie's lamp, no walking on water, no levitation, no ability to manifest riches, no halo over your head, nothing on the outside will be any proof of where you have been on the inside.

We have intrinsic senses: touch, taste, sight, hearing, smell, and another I am calling feeling. At least I recognize it as a sense. These intrinsic senses are like lighthouse beacons that are continuously scanning outward in every direction. Constantly on the alert, recording each moment and in most cases doing a comparison-and-contrast from previously recorded experiences. When your spouse says to you: "Have you seen the car keys?" Immediately, you have a visual recall where you last saw them. "They are on the sink in the bathroom!"

We trust our senses; we pride ourselves if we have an exceptional one or two. We know that when we get old, these senses will diminish in strength. Our eyesight will blur, our hearing gets weaker, and so forth. What we do not realize is that from day one in this life our senses go inwards as well and they do not weaken over time. That's right, inward towards the self. At least this has been my experience. The life you have known has always been outward only. What you probably have always felt out of instinct but never realized is that this life continues inward on an aware stream.

The day you turn to go within is a monumental day; it was for me. Life as you know it will never be the same. Similar to a newborn baby, you feel awkward at first. You are unbalanced, everything seems black. Your sight and senses are just developing and you feel the most vulnerable. Your head tells you to drop all of this nonsense and return to where you were before. But that little voice, the one from the heart, is suddenly emanating a feeling to stay the course. Give it a chance! Give it a little sincere time for the seed to sprout. How long does it take for a tomato seed to sprout? Give your inner garden the same consideration and something wonderful will happen. Something small and significant will sprout that will be your first indicator: "There is another world in here!"

Those senses that have been constantly going out, out, out... turn them to go within, within, within. This is about as easy as turning a stampeding herd of buffalo. My experience; turn them 1 degree, the next day another 1 degree, and the next day 1 degree more. Soon your herd of senses will race inwards and an amazing thing occurs, you recognize that you are feeling with your sight, feeling with your hearing, feeling with your taste, feeling, feeling, and feeling more. One can only cross the landscape within using your feelings in a passionate pursuit to embrace something deeply embedded within you. You will understand how the salmon must feel returning to their origin. What a draw you too will feel to return.

The more you practice going within, the more intoxicating it becomes. The day you realize that your breath contains all that you have ever dreamed; is a marvelous day! Because you have just become the richest person in the world and have the rest of your life to wallow in the sea of appreciation.

The day you somehow sense that life continues within, your first step within becomes a significant day in one's life. Here it is, here is where I need to dwell, and here is where answers come at you without ever asking a question. This last line will not make sense until you experience it. Wow, life returns to that awe-like type of adventure. I found the love I searched for in this world within me. I found the achievement I looked for in this world within. I encourage you to be the first patriot of the Heart. Alas, it will take everything.

FINDING THE ANGRY MAN

(dialogue lifted from a story)

... The Angry Man rises from his seated position and walks across the garden towards the mountain pond nearby, followed by the soldier that has now become silent. The Angry Man stares down where water-life is in full display.

The Angry Man: "Consider the life of a water skimmer." (as he points to one alight on the surface of the water near some reeds). "The bug that scoots over the surface of the water and never gets more than the bottom of his feet wet." The Angry Man continues; "Is there life beneath that bugs' feet?" The soldier nods with an agreement as the Angry Man continues without looking at the soldier. "The enormity of life that lives below him along with the very nature of the life-giving properties of water itself makes the existence of that bug near meaningless in comparison. Near meaningless." He repeats this line. "And yet that bug will never know what is just beneath its feet. Will never know the abundance of life erupting on the other side of that veil."

The Angry Man continues: "We are exactly like that bug. We exist on this side of the veil and are ignorant of the magnitude of Life available to us if we would only break the surface. Life as you know it (making a grand gesture in space) pales in comparison. As vast as you think this life is out here, compared to the life that expands inwardly (making a pinching gesture with his two fingers). Everything you have ever desired lies beneath your feet, little bug, EVERYTHING! And yet you only see the reverse reflection on the surface, and are constantly skimming here and skimming there trying, without success mind you, to acquire what you desire."

"Because you cannot attain your heart's desire, your mind creates an alternative world. Over time, you grow to fit into this alternative world. Replacing feeling with thinking, replacing joy with desires, replacing happiness with duty, and replacing knowing with believing. So, to answer your question 'why do I sit?', I sit because someone with overwhelming kindness revealed a magnificent gift deep within me. Showed me how to step gently on the edge of creation unfolding and swing on the fragrance of Joy. For you to know the true meaning of my words, you need to first find a glimmer who you truly are, then follow the path where only the real YOU can walk and you will find your heart's fulfillment awaiting you." END (this is only a selected scene from a much larger story).

8

I FOUND ANSWERS

Answers to questions I didn't even remember I had. Answers that appeared to reach back years to when I first struggled to form a question. Unraveling. A wonderful phenomenon to feel yourself untangle from self-created shackles that keep you imprisoned. These descriptions are not poetic; they are real. Real enough to torture and torment. I didn't or couldn't see my prison of my making. But I created a good one. One strong enough to keep me blindfolded to the gift of Life. One strong enough that would gladly keep me from ever seeing the light of day. I did not know I was in prison. I did not know I was suffocating. The value of going within unlocks the shackles that bind me to my prison floor. It opens the cell door and allows for the fragrance of true freedom to fill my nostrils. I cannot express enough, the value of going within.

The Kingdom of Heaven is within. When you first heard this phrase, did you assume it was a metaphor? Were you ever told that it represents something other than the location itself? The speaker never intended this to be self-help, feel-good type of expression. The great man who said this was trying to be as clear as he possibly could. We just never realized this was a real destination. Like the water bug, our culture would rather skim over the reflected veil and accept the explanations of scholars. Rather than taking the challenging personal plunge, head first, and discover for ourselves, if Heaven was real or not? Believe over knowing. Which one is freedom?

Knowing something truly requires an enormous amount of effort to rise out of our developed beliefs and discover that sacred territory we possess. We have all the tools to go within regardless if we are blind, deaf, arrogant, or crippled. If a person is still breathing, the path inward is ours to walk. Whoever blocked your way and told you there is no life within is lying to you. Ask anyone who has truly traveled beyond the veil. That inner voice has been begging for us to turn around. It is always feeling in our direction. It is feeling now, consider answering the call.

Words in our vocabulary such as success, freedom, purpose, joy, inner strength, love, accomplishment, are feelings, aren't they? They might reflect a physical accomplishment but without the feeling, no monetary amount will be enough to fill the gaping hole you have within. At least it hasn't for me. As a society, that is exactly what we have done. We have traded Life for money. We pursued anything and everything to get more money. We will endure hardships, separation, criminal acts, and pain to feed greed. We have become slaves by our own admission.

The ideal I am expressing is that there is nothing on the outside I could do to feel an overwhelming sense of completion. Overwhelming is the keyword. I might get a hint of achievement or success or accomplishment but not overwhelming. We find the success we seek within; we find the accomplishment we seek within; we find the joy we seek within, and the love I seek has and will forever be, within.

Another voice once said, Know Thyself. This expression was not intended to become a corporate motivational poster. The great man was trying to encourage others to delve within. For truly to understand, would improve our lives in exponential proportions.

The value of going within is a path to rediscover and reconnect with Life itself. Life is emanating from within you. You can touch it. You can allow Life to touch you. To envelope you. Life has been feeling in your direction for a very long time. I encourage you to turn around and reach for it. Similar to the two birds sitting on a branch.

Imagine if you will, the rotation of an LP record. It takes little knowledge to know the surface rotation is moving the fastest towards the outside of the album. The closer the needle glides towards the center of the album, the slower the surface speed. Do you get that image? Now, imagine this is your mind on steroids moving so fast you are in anguish. You play music loud to drown out the noise in your head, you make a cocktail to take the edge off, and you smoke a puff to chill. The slower your mind works, the easier it is to tolerate the last few hours of the day.

Imagine if you would, placing the needle on the spindle in the center of the turntable. How slow is the rotation now? Very slow, almost still. Placing the needle in the exact center of the spindle, according to physics, there would be no movement at all. We would have replaced chaos with stillness. And stillness gives illumination to clarity. When our minds are still, clarity arrives. You cannot see your reflection on turbulent water, but when water is motionless, silky smooth, you can see yourself perfectly. No different.

The closer you become to the moment of NOW, the remarkable evidence of Life becomes recognizable. I found this clarity to be pristine (the best word to describe it). As if the moment of creation was unfolding before your eyes. There is no such thing as the future. The future is a projection of imagination based on patterns of time that have long passed. The origins of my life ONLY exist in this brief and delicate moment of NOW. I am blind, literally, to the magic that is unfolding under my nose when I am lost in thought. When I am bouncing between the past to the future over to make-believe, with blatant disregard for the present. I might as well be a cartoon character on a bumper sticker. That is how cheap I am treating this gift of life. But when I am tightly embracing this pure moment, without thought of any kind, I become the most fortunate person alive.

The marvel of practicing pulls and directs the pilgrim to a very thin moment in time. Your time. This thin whisper of a moment is only for you. And will never return in the history of creation. With clarity, I have witnessed this phenomenon, and it is priceless. No amount of power or wealth can be compared. With continued practice, this expanse appears to increase (at least it has for me).

A NIGHT IN SANTA CRUZ

I knew a girl that was moving to Northern California who asked if I would drive her car along with her two dogs to Santa Cruz, California (her boyfriend was flying her separately). She knew that I was moving to Monterey (which wasn't far away) so I accepted her offer.

This was my first trip to Northern California, so it was very adventurous for me to discover new surroundings within California. My destination was to meet her somewhere in the Santa Cruz Mountains. If you have ever been in the Santa Cruz Mountains without today's GPS, it is very easy to get lost and especially at night with no streetlights. To my delight, I found the little cabin in the woods. She greeted me at the door and was so happy to become reunited with her dogs. I think those two guys thought they were being abandoned, so when they saw her I became their savior. The dogs and I had become acquainted on our long drive and I felt a little remiss when it came time to say goodbye. Under the moonlight, she invited me in and said I could spend the night here and in the morning she would give me a ride to Monterey.

Upon entering the little one-room cabin, it startled me to see a very attractive young woman lying in an elevated bed. As soon as I had entered the room, she bolted upright to present herself. I think she liked what she saw and whatever the description her girlfriend had given; she was not disappointed. I had seen this interior design layout before using limited space, where the location of the bed was elevated closer to the ceiling improving the warmth. Underneath her elevated bed, she had arranged a beautiful seating area using oversized pillows. It turned out this cabin was not my friends but this girlfriend of hers (the one in bed). They graciously invited me to make myself at home. In my head, I was wondering where would I be sleeping? As quickly as I had arrived, my friend waved goodbye and left with her dogs to be with her boyfriend somewhere else.

No sooner had the door closed when I heard the following words gently wafting down from the elevated bed. "Do you want to smoke a joint?" I think she could see a romantic evening developing. Now, I ask you, how does a young man turn down such an invitation? And yet, I did exactly that. This is no lie.

I thanked her for the offer but expressed that the trip had been long and I would rather crash for the evening. She reluctantly turned off the lights and went back to bed while I immediately sat up to practice on those pillows underneath her. I wasn't sleepy at all; I was on a mission.

For a prolonged period now whenever I relaxed to practice, I was traveling easily. Everything was new to me and all I wanted to do was continue this acceleration inwards. I was being showered with a love I had never felt before. Every practice session was opening new domains, and it was incredibly intoxicating. The idea to trade what I was experiencing for sex and drugs was not even a hard decision.

Wow! What a good choice that turned out to be! That evening started a love affair I have never left. In my practice that very evening, sitting there on those oversized pillows, in that darkened cabin I went so very deep and became surrounded by an experience (only words I can use). When suddenly; time stopped. This practice session became the first time I separated from my chattering mind. All at once, as if by falling inwards, BOOM, it all stopped. In one instant, I felt a separation, a real separation. This resulted in a mixture of tremendous grounding (best words to use) along with a pristine stillness.

This deafening stillness continued without interruption for hours. As if someone had lifted a very large power generator off of my back. Silence... a silence that felt like an atmosphere. A separation of such magnitude that I was in a state of both amazement and gratitude. I felt like I was standing in the heart of stillness. The ever-moving, hectic, noisy mind of mine had left the building.

I was not expecting this to happen; I didn't even know this experience was possible. For the first time, I was living in the moment called NOW. My senses were off the hook. I was not delving into the past or escaping into the future. I was not inside or outside. It was neither daytime nor nighttime for me. That part of what you thought was an integral part of you was an aberration. I felt so grounded and free. I am the breath and it is very aware of me.

I wondered if I could remain in this state if I opened my eyes. Ever so slowly I lifted my eyelids to the darkened room lit only by the moonlight streaming in through the windows as I silently erupted inside. A love that was so extreme and priceless was churning and growing with every breath. My every sense was dancing. I felt I could detect every hair on my tingling body. I would not let go. It was so thick as if the substance of the present brought reality. My teacher became my master that evening and in many ways my friend.

The love we are looking for is within inside of us. When

you separate yourself from the battering of your mind, you walk through the veil into heaven... no lie.

For me, this is where true meditation BEGINS. For me, this is the state of being where prayers become communication. This is where Life lives and you are welcome. Past, future, and make-believe are phantoms. The real environment for living is in this incredible place so thin that one thought and you are back in the storm. Life becomes anew all over again when there is no war raging in your head. I always wondered if this was the place where the saying "being born again" originated. Here it is, hidden in plain sight. This realm of clarity has been with me my whole life and I never could see it. Right under my nose this whole time.

This is as far as I want to describe this location. I feel if I continue, I will only add concepts and consequences to your journey. I will tell you with all honesty that YES it exists and that for you too it will be as if you made the return trip to Eden. You accomplished what Adam and Eve wanted to do so many eons ago.

It requires constant vigilance, although it gets to where your heart will remind you when you are drifting because the separation from the present becomes agonizing. Answers come at you all day to questions you never asked. It sounds strange, but the feeling is euphoric. The more I learn, the less I know. True wisdom is to waft in the breeze of kindness.

Your sleep becomes a continuation of clarity and if you dream, at least for me, becomes parables for you to learn more. The secret of Joy is that there is no secret. What did I do to deserve this kind of blessing? My humility is my only true clothing, wear it well.

I celebrated the following day as if it was Christmas morning and the world was my present. I was having a pure experience of living. I felt my breathing had become deeper overnight as if my lungs could expand twice their normal size. I felt a pressure on my chest had been lifted. I was ripped! I was locked in the moment of now and could see life blooming before me. Could I continue this state of being? Why yes, I can.

9

HOW DOES ONE GO WITHIN and WHY?

To answer the question for 'why' think of it this way. Every time you see a tree, you can't see its roots, can you? And yet, without deep roots, this tree is susceptible to an unfruitful life in more ways than one.

There is a eucalyptus tree in my neighborhood that I pass on my daily dog walks. It sprouted on the border of a neighbor's yard and the city sidewalk. No one really took any ownership of the tree and so it sprouted and grew close to five feet tall before someone thought otherwise and they cut it down. What they neglected to do was remove the roots. Within 6 months that tree had grown multiple trunks and was again overhead and very healthy, all by itself.

Once again, the happy eucalyptus was cut down. And once again the roots, which had grown even deeper, remained. Today, there is a small grove that towers over the sidewalk.

The analogy is obvious, without going deep and out of

sight; one doesn't secure Life for one's self. We, as a culture, do not extend any value towards the riches that live within. There is no mention or awareness that something like this exists. Or to value having one's roots embedded into the core of Life is possible. For this reason alone, the question of why is a moot point.

To answer the question of how does one go within is more challenging. This will be a challenge because in our culture we never ask for help, we are privileged and we can do anything and everything by ourselves. "No thanks, I can do it myself. I'm sure there is a YouTube video that can teach me." Adios amigo.

Another, even more, difficult challenge is finding the proper teacher that can truly help. You will need your heart to discern the actor from the real. There are plenty of fake ones parading as the real deal. I feel their intentions are genuine but their motives are askew. You only need to search on Google to see the magnitude of personalities waiting eagerly to help you. All of them with great credentials and pedigree. Facilitators and social media influencers will only add to the confusion. Books upon books, spewing their realizations for you to believe and follow.

Look for the person who can show you the doorway to the self. I will not tell you who my teacher is (could be male or female). Possibly by the time you read this book, both my teacher and I will have passed on. This book is to inspire you to turn towards Life and discover the connection Life has imbued you with. Life will always have an ambassador ready. As much as you are looking for your teacher, I tell you, your teacher is making significantly more effort to find you.

The magic between teacher and student is what poets make epic stories from. Yours will not be any different. To find the teacher do what I did; ask for help with all the humility and sincerity you have. You might wonder in what direction should one ask? My question to you is; where do you feel you need to ask? You can answer this question yourself by now, can't you? I am confident that if you are sincere, you and your teacher will soon meet. Life is conscious of you. Ask, and stay alert to what happens next. This isn't hocus pocus.

The first step should lead you towards humility. Enough to recognize you need help to accomplish this endeavor. This person is, in fact, the one individual that can get you to the threshold of yourself. This was a very scary moment for me (maybe not for you). I had listened to several individuals who performed admirably in their disguise as someone exceptional and worthy of my trust. But my inner voice never responded until I heard about the one that started me on my path within. My inner voice was on fire when I listened to the words from this person. On fire. Lean on your heart to guide you and remember it will be a feeling that will be voiced.

What you are about to do is challenging and will take everything you are willing to put forth. Before you can see your way properly, you will stumble your way forward. Don't be discouraged. The beacon you will use to navigate is this feeling of the heart. That little voice will become more recognizable through practice. Develop your inner feeling. No plant in your garden sprouted from seed overnight. How long did it take for your tomato plants to break the soil's surface? How long before the first fruit appeared? You would be wise to use nature as an indicator of the length it will take for you to see results.

Your inner discoveries through practicing will not be noticeable to anyone else (think of them as your roots). Your teeth will not get whiter, or the hair on your head begins to grow again. You won't be able to do magic tricks for your friends, but you will discover something wonderful for yourself! Something incredibly wonderful!

Set your own pace. This is nothing like you have ever attempted before. The awakening of yourself is a discovery. Initially, you will have enthusiasm, and I encourage you to use this inspirational rush for your benefit. Practice as much as you feel compelled and return to practice when you feel to do so. There are no time constraints and no restrictions on the time of day to practice.

Practicing at first will feel awkward (at least it was for me, maybe not you). Harnessing your mind is comical at first as you notice how it erupts all over the place. It is these thoughts that keep you buoyant, stuck on the surface so to speak, but give it some time, practice with purpose, practice developing your inner FEELINGS. You haven't used them for a long time and you will need to develop this kind of strength.

When you find a feeling, hold on to it, see where it leads you. Remember, everything you discover within you is YOU. You will need to remind yourself of this later on but for now, embrace your inner feelings because your inner feelings will help you realize that you are NOT your thoughts. This last line I just wrote is a pivotal understanding. YOU are not your thoughts even though they are barking inside your head. For now, embark on a path of discovery and know that no explorer discovered unknown lands without leaving something behind. We need to leave our thoughts behind, our doubts behind, and our fears behind. This will be difficult at first.

Your teacher will give you the means to turn your attention from the outer to the inner. Put the instructions to test and sit furiously. How much attention would you give a seedling if your survival depended on this seed to sprout? It will require an enormous amount of sincerity to put forth. The Kingdom of Heaven is within. No one ever said it would be easy to attain. If they did, then they are lying. If you are desperate to reach the heart, the silence of this breath becomes a precious ladder to reach your destiny.

The doorway seems to be the same for everyone, but the path is unique to you alone. You will chart your journey. No one else can do it for you and anyone else's map will not work for you so even though you are reading this little book about my experience (this is my map and not yours), it is unique, only for me.

Your map reveals YOU and you alone. You can't push this on your kids or expect your significant other to embrace it. You are the navigator, captain, and crewman. Take care of your vessel and it will care for you. Raise your sails high; it is the only way to capture and enjoy the winds of grace. No sails, no grace. No effort, no gain.

It took me a while to trust my inner self (my heart). I thought meditation would have a different result (add your concepts here). What it showed me was something different and way beyond my wildest imaginations. It takes time, no different from a farmer preparing for a new season. If you want to taste the fruits of your efforts, begin by preparing the soil to accept the seed. This small seed needs all the attention you can give. With a consistent effort, over time, it will bear fruit for you to enjoy. It is that simple.

I feel this path within takes courage. You are going against the grain of society. A society and culture that expects you to perform a particular way. This path requires your complete commitment, not at first, but after you see results it will confront you with the reality that to go deeper will require an element of selfless participation. You are exploring uncharted territory that will require clarity to navigate. Persistent perseverance prevails and anything short of this resolute will not bear fruit.

Life is a jealous lover and is so committed to me that the expectation is that I will commit to Life in kind. If you want to hear the Breath of Life, you need to be all here and what a beautiful sound it is. You are as rare as a snowflake and everything about your life is precious and wonderful. Your priceless life will develop the deeper you progress within.

MONTANA

I had a friend who was an avid skydiver. She was describing to me her experience the first time she did a Halo jump (higher than 30,000 feet). At that high altitude, you need to breathe oxygen on the way up in the jump plane and she wanted to see how far she could maintain clarity before she needed oxygen (youth; we are so indestructible).

So up she goes with the others, feeling a dash of bravado. As the jump plane flew higher and higher, she continued to access her faculties and was feeling she must be some kind of exceptional human because she couldn't detect any changes. The plane had crossed the 20,000 ft. level and was proceeding to 30,000 ft. Well, nothing appeared any different. She was way above altitude height but felt immune to the altitude change and imagined that she probably could hike to the base of Everest.

Everyone was looking at her and began asking how she felt with grins (as if they knew something she didn't). She told the others she felt fine. She felt strong, alert, and breathing was easy. Then one of them responded by saying: "Look at your fingernails" upon realizing they had turned a deep color of blue. One person held up a compact mirror and said look at the color in your lips (which were also blue).

With this alarm, she reached for a face-mask and took a hit of oxygen while looking out the window towards the ground below. Wham! Just like that, color rushed back into the land. She wasn't even aware that color was no longer in her sight. With another inhale, her senses were returning and her thinking became clearer as the other jumpers only laughed at her.

This genuine story represents what happens to us when we sit and practice (although in reverse). We are in an altered state of mind thousands of feet from the ground. We think all is well and those around us support our delusional mind because they too are suffering from altitude poisoning. So it begins and at first, it feels kind of exciting thinking to yourself; I am meditating. As if you are expecting some miracle to happen. You sit and sit; you go through your practice session and then you get up. Gee, nothing happened. The next day, you do it again and with the same results. The next day, the next day, the next day and you feel you could go either way with this thing until you curiously surprise yourself walking in a park, or out with friends when you comment to yourself; "Wow, what a beautiful moment" and while you are taking in the strikingly crisp clarity, it hits you. "Is it beautiful? Or am I just feeling a beautiful experience?" You look around and notice, Holy Shit! It's me! I am the one who is having a beautiful day! Maybe I should put more consideration into this thing than I thought? As I descended from my lofty heights towards the center of myself; color is returning, my senses are enriched, and clarity is growing. Thoughts in my head have gone silent. This wasn't what I thought meditation would bring. And yet way beyond my expectations.

Practicing is like scuba diving. If you never tried scuba diving, the buoyancy from your wetsuit and the full tank of air makes it relatively challenging to start a dive. Watching beginners as they helplessly struggle to begin their dive is fun to watch. They kick and flail but remain on the surface until they manage, with a lot of effort, to get about three feet under, at which point the water pressure on the body makes their descent easy.

I found it surprising one day during my practice, with some conviction, that I was experiencing being within. As shallow as it was, it was a genuine discovery, not a belief. The awareness of this internal realm wasn't a mystery; it felt natural and somewhat expected. Had I been here before and forgotten? Why does this feel so natural? Can I stay in here for hours? It feels like I could. I never knew my breath contained everything within it. Absolutely everything!

When you first start practicing, allow yourself to travel

within the best way that you can. Never practice with a clock. You are not baking a cake; you are discovering yourself within. You are developing your inner strengths. Like a baby, you will be unbalanced at first. Sit for as long as you feel comfortable. This isn't religious and doesn't require you to endure pain. Practice from your heart. I would tell myself that "I am searching for YOU, show me the way." And then pay attention.

Take a step at a time, embrace the feeling, and separate yourself from thought. If my thoughts request we get up from our practice and do something else, I will tell my mind; "No, you go do that... I am just going to sit here a little more." Oddly, it works most of the time as if this mind has its own agenda. That is when it feels more and more like a parasite that lives off its host.

Before I go to bed, I sit for as long as I can before I fall asleep. Regardless of the length. In my experience, I feel remarkably rested with the limited hours I slept. And what about those dreams?! Oh my God! Only those who dive get the pearls. I implore you to take your initial enthusiasm and dive deep. It is in this depth where you will have your first taste of knowing over believing. Knowing doesn't go away.

If you convince yourself that this was a nice experiment, but you have decided to put this meditation thing on the shelf until you have more free time to dedicate to it. You will float all the way back to the surface and back up into the clouds. All those experiences will only be a fond memory; suitable material at dinner parties or school reunions. It is in the consistency that will prevail. Does your breath put you on the shelf until your vacation comes around? I hope not, but if you want fulfillment, gain it and then go deeper still.

Who finds fantastic surf? Who finds superb sushi? Who finds gold? Only those who seek what they are looking for will find it. Consider these last three lines; if you want to find great surf, you will probably need to travel a significant distance to find the waves you are looking for. If you value incredible sushi, I am sure you need to do some searching to find it. If you are a prospector for gold, you need to dig deep. These examples express that one needs to leave their current location if they want the rewards of their effort. No difference in your journey within.

During practice, it surprises me every time I experience an unraveling of myself from tangles and knots I never knew I was tied-up in. Mental ones. Knots and tangles of confusion, of concepts and cultural stigmas. Letting go of those buoyant buoys will allow you to descend even deeper. I didn't even have to make an effort letting go of those buoys. In my practice... boom, I realize the buoy of confusion when it is floating away. Talking to myself, I will say; "Why was I holding on to that for this long?"

I have always delighted in allowing myself to become saturated with the NOW (an excellent way to put it). After one morning's session, making breakfast before I had to get on the highway for work, I was standing over the kitchen counter when I realized I was in Love! That feeling of ambrosia (if ambrosia could have a feeling) bubbling up and filling my apartment. That intoxicating feeling of joy mixed with love, when it hit me... I wasn't dating anyone! I had no lover. I was single and was only preparing breakfast. But I was IN LOVE.

What a powerful moment. An incredible moment of freedom to recognize that I have the origin of love within me. This thick feeling will not leave me. This fragrance of love will always be with me, and mine to indulge.

TRUE ART

The greatest art is living
To be conscious of every second
To appreciate every moment
To constantly exchange confusion for clarity
It cannot be hung on a wall,
Recorded and shared
It gets no applause
Only I know and enjoy its success
It is the most difficult art form
Yet the most rewarding
Any other art is
Only an expression
Of the one true art
-Carla Cahill

There were the times where it was quiet, dead quiet... expansive and black. I called this walking in the desert. Alone in the dark can sometimes remind you of proverbs straight out of the scriptures. I thought of the Jews walking in the desert for forty years and wondered if they meant this desert? Because it sure feels like a desert and the only thing I feel is happening is my sense of feeling is improving. Through this desert of darkness, I can feel some worthy attribute on the other side. Love the desert, your sense of feeling increases with every step.

I approach practicing focused and determined as possible. On most occasions, the time spent feels as easy as gliding on a stream inward. On other days, it feels like I am holding a chariot of dragons just to maintain my ground. The more I practice, the easier and richer it becomes. My inner senses heighten and joy fills my being. The source of joy is within, and you can become drunk with repeated indulgences. Humility will serve you well. You will never be humble, intolerant.

I need to remind you that many of you received a gift a very long time ago. You only need to plant the seed and tend to your garden for the length it takes to grow tomatoes to see something remarkable. It will amaze you. For me, my ability to notice the change was as subtle as that skydiver who refused oxygen (but in reverse). The more I practiced, the more of Life I could see. Hidden in plain sight.

I love to sit. I feel very lucky. The periods where I have been sick with the flu or with a cold suck. I expect little more than securing my place. This ability to go within is a very personal experience. It has been so far. Inside is where the heart lives and being in that company makes life a magnificent gift. It takes constant desire with an ingredient of fortitude. Going within becomes communion with a reassuring companion. Enjoy the company.

There you are, alone in the dark and it never felt so complete. You truly feel you are not alone and the host is benevolent. Dive deep young adventurer, do not listen to the winds of doubt. Keep your head down and dive deep. There is no end to these wondrous depths. I encourage everyone, please dive deep.

It has been my privilege to have received the Gift so many years ago in my youth. I needed peace, and it has provided me with that, and so much more. The first time I heard someone speak of the possibility to receive this gift, I sat for over an hour glued to every word. However, the speaker would sometimes ask those in the room if they had understood what he had said, and I realized I could remember nothing of what had been spoken. As someone who prided himself on having a fairly flawless memory, this puzzled me for quite a while.

My understanding of this now is simple. My heart is engaged when someone is speaking from their heart about this gift and it is not the words but the feeling of the heart that is engaging me. Politicians know what words to use but are lost to the experience behind them. I am fortunate that I don't rely on words but can feel my heart through the practice of the Gift every day. For me, this keeps the heart closer to the surface so I can readily experience and communicate about the heart when the time is right. I need to live in my heart as much as possible. I need to be its humble servant and to the teacher who gave me this gift, a humble student.

All I have to say is to experience the heart, practice the Gift, and go see the great person. Everyone wants an incredible life, don't you? If you follow the feeling of these words, I guarantee that you will have an incredible one. I surely have.

- Brad G.

When I was in high school, I had an English teacher that approached literature from so many perspectives with so much enthusiasm and humor he instantly became the most sought-after teacher to have; I included. All the brainiacs in school petitioned to take his classes, which created a wave of jealousy among the other teachers. I was not a brainiac; I wasn't even a good student. I did everything I could to keep myself out of the cellar. I struggled in his class, but I had never been so creatively challenged before in any class. I never worked harder for a 'C' (you probably can tell by how poorly I have written this book).

He was demanding, relentless, and forward-thinking. He loved literature in any form one could find literature. From verses in the scriptures to ads for cigarettes, from Beatles lyrics to battle hymns. For a high school class, he was so over the top that everyone felt he was destined for greatness. Sure enough, he left the high school level for the university level after two years and never looked back.

An exceptional teacher can bring illumination to an unlit room. Similarly, a teacher of the heart can reveal a wonderment with unlimited proportions for you. This area is unfamiliar to you, and you would be wise to use humility as a student of the heart. The teacher will never be what you expected and yet beyond your expectations.

His or her importance? They introduce the doorway so you can begin your return. In your life, they will relentlessly inspire you to know yourself. They will also if you get the chance to spend time with them, confront the hell out of you. One moment they will do something or say something as close to perfection as your little mind can perceive and then at other times, you will want to compare their actions to a trucker at a way-station in Texas. It will confuse you to no end trying to link the two together. My advice, abandon trying to make some sense out of it. You'll only start up an infinite number of "whys", only to sweep you away into the river of befuddlement.

My relationship with my teacher is unique. My teacher and I are not close and I have only seen my teacher speak in person on rare occasions. This comment might have surprised you. The times I have had the opportunity have always benefited me immensely. It doesn't matter to me where I am seated in the room, only that I am in the room. For me, my teacher captures my heart in seconds and then slows time itself. What my teacher says makes my ears pang because I have waited for years to hear such words. I have learned so much over time from listening to this noble person speak about Life. I pay great attention to the wisdom that is shared for sure as the sun will rise, I will apply what my teacher is expressing in the coming year.

I have kept my description of my teacher short on purpose. As unique as you are reflects the uniqueness of your relationship with the one who will reveal the doorway to your true self. Your teacher will not fight your battles, but they will gladly drive your chariot, although you need to request their help and their help is imperative. Your relationship will be a personal one, a magical one. The teacher becomes something more significant when the student crosses a personal threshold within and makes a discovery for themselves that is incredible. This happened for me and from that point forward my teacher became my Master. No and's, if's' or but's about it.

I am eternally grateful for this gift that has been shown to me. Reality and knowing will always crush the snot out of make-believe and believing every day of the year.

10

A GREAT GIFT IS HIDDEN IN PLAIN SIGHT

It was never intended to be hidden, but along the way, we lost sight of it a long time ago. This powerful resource that has been misplaced is directly under one's nose, but we don't perceive it. The inherent value of this resource and what it can do for us is unmeasurable. The memory loss of this gift has resulted in our inability to see for ourselves the value of Life itself. No Bueno!

Imagine you are traveling on a bullet train exceeding 300 mph. Your window seat gives you a splendid view of the scenery zooming by. Imagine you open the window (just pretend okay). The windstorm and hurricane sound would be death-defying, wouldn't it? How much peace is available at that moment? And yet this is exactly how we live our lives. Maybe we are not moving at 300 mph, but our minds surely are. Our minds move so fast and loud we have lost our sense of smell. Don't believe me? Wherever you are (at this moment) describe to yourself what you can smell? Probably nothing; smells like air. Just air, with no distinguishable currents either. Probably not one hint of the fragrance of life, nothing? You probably cannot discern moisture in the air as well... can you?

If I have lost one sense, how many other faculties have I lost? How would I even know if I was missing any (remember the skydiver girl)? This is what it's like when we are moving at 300 mph in our minds. But when you decelerate, over time you notice things you didn't before. You notice a lot of things you didn't know existed. Fragrances, temperatures, colors, textures, sounds, and feelings fill your awareness. Keep slowing down until you come to a complete stop. What do you hear? What can you see? What do you smell? And how deep can you feel? How much peace is available now? Like night and day. Like night and day, just saying.

Could this be Heaven? Could all of this be the actual Garden of Eden? Could this be the very place we want to go to after we die? What is missing for it to be Heaven? _____ (place your answer here). And if you were to discover your answer, then this would be Heaven, correct? If you, yourself, contained the very answer you wrote, what does that make this place? What does that make you? Hidden in plain sight is not a poet's gest. It is a call to action.

Everyone wants to go to Heaven, but no one wants to die. I have said this earlier and I feel the importance to repeat it again. All living creatures cling to life with a forceful grip. Something within all of us values being alive. Everything alive is breathing, don't you find that odd? One breath and the creature has life, last breath and the creature ceases to exist. How valuable is this breath? Where does it come from? How would you discover the importance of this breath for yourself?

I am old enough to remember technology that is no longer in use because we have replaced it with something superior. We replaced vacuum tubes with transistors; we replaced transistors with integrated circuitry and tomorrow's technology will move information a zillion times faster than the vacuum tubes. If someone was trying to communicate with you using Morse code over the wire, would you receive it? Never.

Now imagine someone was trying to communicate with you that was using an instrument that was far superior to anything we have now. Again, we would never know it. Our capacity to receive awareness is so small, it hardly registers in our history books. Imagine that your breath contained an enormous capacity of understanding. That contained within the very element that is keeping you alive was also the communication link to tap something remarkable. Unless you alter your awareness, this vital stream of wisdom and mercy will go unnoticed. I am the tuner that needs fine-tuning. Tune to the frequency of this breath and witness who is calling.

As a teenager, I felt that the person I wanted to meet, and perhaps have a relationship with, would do similar things that I liked. They would probably be in the same location as me, experiencing similar events. If I surfed, they would probably enjoy surfing. If I liked a particular musical band, we might bump into each other at the same concert. What I didn't realize at the time was the love I was hoping to meet was already with me. The love you are looking for is living within you. They have always been there and will be your companion that will accompany you on, after the last breath. This last sentence is only my feeling, so don't believe it.

For me, this is the love I have waited for all my life. It is beyond deep, richer than rich, kinder than kindness. What a grace to have such love and support. Although to feel Love's presence, you need to be in that whisper of a state where Love lives.

Many of you probably have a dog? My dog loves me regardless if I have shaved or taken a shower. If I'm fat or looking beautiful. Unconditional love at any hour of the day. My dog just loves being with me (she goes to work with me every day). When I return from a trip or a quick trip to the market, she greets me as if I am the most important person in the entire world and showers me with love and attention.

This is how I feel the love within feels about me. The love within can surround me, embrace me, express a joy I cannot explain. The most wonderful element is that I am FEELING the love. My love comes from such a deep place. I feel like a sailor who has willingly jumped overboard in pursuit of a mermaid. I needed to dive deep to find this love, but when I did, I haven't let go. Embrace the love and surrender to the depth. Writing these words is the first time I have ever expressed this phenomenon.

The love of my life is LIFE, waiting, and yearning for me to come home. Who is the love of your life? Your Life is the love. One needs to embrace the driver of the car to understand this important wisdom. Keep your life simple, choose kindness even in a spouse.

Several years ago, I was at a corporate dinner in Osaka, Japan. The company I represented were the publishers of a computer game this team in Japan produced. Seated at this dinner table are all the senior managers from both companies responsible for the success of the game. The president from the Osaka team was at the head of the table and our host. The dialogue had been light and friendly when the president presented a question to the group. "If you had this life to do over, what would you want to be?" He then quickly followed the question by saying he would have liked to be a professional baseball player and then addressed the woman seated to his left to go next and speak her dream life.

There must have been twelve of us at this table and I was probably the eighth person in line to describe what profession would be my dream to have. When my turn came, after hearing stories of actors, musicians, and professional sports I said sincerely, "I would like my life all over again. This current one, as simple as it has been, I would love to live this life all over again without hesitation."

A hush came over the table and I immediately thought to myself, "You moron, should have said, professional surfer." I had answered sincerely. I truly have had one of those storybook lives. Even with the awful years, I would pay good money to have this life all over again. My response had caught everyone off-guard, and I didn't know how to continue. The next person in line was staring at me, speechless.

In that awkward moment, our Japanese host (the president) knowing me to be an honest and talented contributor to the success of their game, he took back the control of the tables' discussion, and for the next few hours, I wished I had recorded the conversations that followed. It was as if we permitted ourselves to speak honestly without fear of judgment. The president opened with such a raw story of his own life, which led others in the table to do likewise. We shared one remarkable life story after another among strangers. I feel we hide from ourselves in plain sight. If we would only have courage, we would see that everyone is discovering their incredible life. We hide in fear and welcome the "All Clear" shout for us to come out of our shells.

I am struck by the importance of equality, of all things. Good, bad, strong, weak, black, white, push, pull, sweet, sour. The acceptance of all things in juxtaposition to an appreciation for one thing. You cannot have one without the whole. Eliminating one thing would consequently damage all things. Every one thing exists and depends on all things. You must have all things to have the one. You must embrace one thing to safely protect all things.

After my first sign of awareness, I began practicing with a force. I had my first taste of this unknown land and I wanted more. After a brief spell, I recognized impressions that were not wondrous and beautiful but discomforting. It became increasingly painful to sit while I was being confronted with a barrage of memories and visuals that marked my most ugly. Images and recollections from my past born of selfishness, hubris, and ignorance had come back to haunt my sessions.

Regardless of how painful it becomes, endure it, learn from it, and embrace it, because it is YOU, or it used to be you. Take heart this will pass, don't hide from your life, embrace it, accept it, and learn from what Life is trying to teach and reveal to you. What I learned from this was that for the rest of my life, my unconscious acts will confront me and I need to take full responsibility for them. Bury nothing, hide from nothing and attempt to sow the seeds that will bear me fruit and avoid planting those seeds that will become obstacles later on. I will have to reap what I sow.

This sounds so common sense, and yet we are so uncommon. I look at it this way. I am filled with the impurities of this life and I have no problem making more mistakes. But if I truly choose well, I can avoid obstacles that at first bring temporary pleasure for a lifetime of misery and regret. We are the ones who plant the obstacles in this path of life. "What doesn't kill me will make me stronger" is a false statement. Some obstacles are handed down as family heirlooms. "Every man in our family has done the same for countless generations! So must you!" It will take courage to walk this path.

WHAT IF I COULD SEE LIFE?

(Designed to be a visual poem)

Try to imagine that you could see life entering this world–show birth of a child in slow motion, showing the doctors and mother and husband (tasteful perspective). Show brand new animal babies, bird eggs hatching, penguins, and giraffes. Using light to illuminate the obvious, as if there was an eruption of light highlighting the recent creation.

Try to imagine that you could see the life-force pulsing in this world. Show the obvious difference from the objects created by man and those that nature created. Using techniques in color design, visual effects, and sound design for emotional gain. See the breath in all things.

Try to imagine the joy and the innocence of childhood, remained long into adulthood. Show scenes of wonders both large and small. The blowhole in Tahiti, snowboarding, sailing, northern lights, grandparents with a twinkle of mischievousness, perhaps other cultures where their faces shine.

Try to imagine that you could stop your mind from screaming and see life unfolding for the first time before your eyes. Show people in a park setting with words rotating over their heads that suddenly dissolved, allowing them to be here in the present. Show people sleeping peacefully.

Imagine that all the love you have ever wanted is within inside of you. Show a close-up of a young woman in a state of harmony.

Imagine all of this to be true.

Fade to black, End.

11

LAST CHAPTER

I have been writing this book for years using simple sheets of paper to capture my awareness and personal epiphanies. I recognize from experience that my understanding is in a constant state of change. Life is always growing and changing. It might resemble the timelessness of a giant redwood tree, but it too is still evolving. Embrace your evolution.

I would like to leave you with these parting words of inspiration. Living in the moment without any thoughts does in fact exist. Only those who look will find. Only those who dive get the pearls and you are never alone, even in your darkest hour. Life is conscious of you, introduce yourself. Now that you have finished my book, consider leaving it somewhere for others to stumble across, such as coffee houses, park benches, bus stops, or wherever someone who has been harboring a feeling but never had words to express, will find this book and be glad.

Thanks for reading,
T.A. Mann

My Whisper

A voice to my friends.

Before the coming of events cascade onto the shore like the last wave of the day; before the sound of many birds fade away into the distance; before the last pitter-patter of rain ceases to fall; let me express to you without constraint or resolve my gratitude and appreciation for your company on this journey of life.

I have had a great time. When you compare my life to historical events, I had more fun. I enjoyed the coming and going of this breath as no one has. It has been a moving tapestry of delight from childhood to now. Colors, music, temperatures, feelings, emotions, tastes, fears, attachments, detachments, loves, and sorrows collectively flowing from my paintbrush of life. I want to thank you.

You were all mirrors reflecting my existence. I saw myself through you. It was because of you that motivated me to attempt the things that I did. All of you. All of you were the cacophony of the celebration of life. All of your voices were instruments performing wonderfully. Joys and hopes and efforts and cares and fears, all of it together transformed a handful of dirt into a living, breathing, caring human being, me. If not for you.

There was one of you that showed me the value of my breath. Revealed the golden core you did. With my effort, I was allowed to embrace this sacred moment and it is everything. I have already thanked you personally. I thank you once more.

I have been lucky but perhaps I was luckier than most. I can feel color, I can feel my sight, I can feel what I hear, I can feel my taste and I can feel within me. No different than floating on the surface of the water face up, and with the gentleness of rotating ones' head, I turned within and could descend into the thickness of life. Surrounded by life, with the added pressure the deeper I descend. I experienced life so very deeply. Deep, deep I floated inward, into the realm of life I go. What a wondrous feeling, what depth to discover. I am the most fortunate. This is the prayer, only I can make. No one alive or in history can make this same prayer. I am the only one. A raindrop falling.

T.A Mann – April 6, 2020, 5:58 pm sitting in the sunroom of my house. It is raining outside. What a beautiful day.

Posted on www.whisperwe.com a site to post your last words.

T.A. Mann met his teacher when he was nineteen years old. In the beginning, he will confess he had doubts until he made a personal commitment to journey inward on a furious path of discovery. To stand in the presence of one's heart is a momentous occasion. This experience along elevates the appreciation of the teacher significantly. T.A. Mann is new to writing. This is his first book on the subject of the self. This new landscape has only begun to emerge on his horizon and he eagerly embraces this new frontier.

Connecting with T.A. Mann
Website: www.raindropfalling.com
Email: tamann@raindropfalling.com

www.ingramcontent.com/pod-product-compliance
Lightning Source LLC
Chambersburg PA
CBHW021127080526
44587CB00012B/1172